Tongue Twisters

Friendly Frank flips fine flapjacks.

COMPILED BY PAM ROSENBERG • ILLUSTRATED BY BOB OSTROM

The Child's World®

Special thanks to Katie Cottrell for her
assistance in compiling source materials.

Published by The Child's World®
1980 Lookout Drive • Mankato, MN 56003-1705
800-599-READ • www.childsworld.com

Acknowledgments
The Child's World®: Mary Berendes, Publishing Director
The Design Lab: Design
Jody Jensen Shaffer: Editing

ISBN 9781626870000
LCCN 2013947280

Printed in the United States of America
Mankato, MN
November, 2013
PA02196

A fly and a flea in a flue were imprisoned, so what could they do? Said the fly, "Let us flee!" "Let us fly!" said the flea. And they flew through the flaw in the flue. Said the flea to the fly as he flew through the flue, "There's a flaw in the floor of the flue." Said the fly to the flea as he flew through the flue, "A flaw in the floor of the flue doesn't bother me. Does it bother you?"

Ann Anteater ate Andy Alligator's apples, so angry Andy Alligator ate Ann Anteater's ants.

How high would a horsefly fly if a horsefly would fly high?

Big black bugs bleed blue black blood but baby black bugs bleed blue blood.

The blue bluebird blinks.

Mares eat oats, and does eat oats, but little lambs eat ivy. A kid'll eat ivy too, wouldn't you?

The cat catchers can't catch caught cats.

As the roaring rocket rose, the restless roosters rollicked.

Cows graze in droves on grass that grows on grooves in groves.

A big black bug bit a big black bear, made the big black bear bleed blood.

BY THE SEA

Sally's selfish selling shellfish, so Sally's shellfish seldom sell.

Pooped purple pelicans.

There was a young fisher named Fischer, who fished for a fish in a fissure. The fish with a grin pulled the fisherman in. Now they're fishing the fissure for Fischer.

A noisy noise annoys an oyster.

HOLIDAYS

Which is the witch that wished the wicked wish?

I wish to wish the wish you wish to wish, but if you wish the wish the witch wishes, I won't wish the wish you wish to wish.

A ghost's sheets would soon shrink in such suds.

Each Easter Eddie eats eighty Easter eggs.

Amidst the mists and coldest frosts, with stoutest wrists and loudest boasts, he thrusts his fist against the posts and still insists he sees the ghosts.

AT SCHOOL

I can't stand when it's written rotten.

Literally literary literature.

White eraser? Right away, sir!

A tutor who tooted a flute died to tutor two tooters to toot. Said the two to the tutor, "Is it harder to toot, or to tutor two tooters to toot?"

The boy blinked at the blank bank blackboard.

Pick a partner and practice passing, for if you pass proficiently, perhaps you'll play professionally.

He threw three free throws.

Purple paper people.

FOOD AND COOKING

Peter Piper picked a peck of pickled peppers. A peck of pickled peppers Peter Piper picked. If Peter Piper picked a peck of pickled peppers, how many pickled peppers did Peter Piper pick?

The cute cookie cutters cut cute cookies. Did the cute cookie cutters cut cute cookies? If the cute cookie cutters cut cute cookies, where are the cute cookies the cute cookie cutters cut?

Blake the baker bakes black bread.

An oyster met an oyster, and they were oysters two. Two oysters met two oysters, and they were oysters, too. Four oysters met a pint of milk and they were oyster stew.

A canner exceedingly canny, one morning remarked to his granny, "A canner can can anything that he can, but a canner can't can a can, can he?"

Crisp crusts crackle crunchily.

Betty Botter bought a bit of butter. "But," said she, "this butter's bitter. If I put it in my batter, it will make my batter bitter. But a bit of better butter that would make my batter better." So Betty Botter bought a bit of better butter, and she put it in her bitter batter and made her bitter batter a bit better.

Does double bubble gum double bubble?

PLACES/TRAVEL

We surely shall see the sun shine soon.

Beautiful babbling brooks bubble between blossoming banks.

Thieves seize skis.

Betty and Bob brought back blue balloons from the big bazaar.

A bloke's back bike brake block broke.

About Bob Ostrom:

Bob Ostrom has been illustrating children's books for nearly twenty years. A graduate of the New England School of Art & Design at Suffolk University, Bob has worked for such companies as Disney, Nickelodeon, and Cartoon Network. He lives in North Carolina with his wife, Melissa, and three children, Will, Charlie, and Mae.

About Pam Rosenberg:

Pam Rosenberg is a former junior high school teacher and corporate trainer. She currently works as a author, editor, and the mother of Sarah and Jake. She took on this project as a service to all her fellow parents of young children. At least now their kids will have lots of jokes to choose from when looking for the one they will tell their parents over and over and over again!